Kyrgyzstan
Bishkek and Tien Shan
Stephen Platt

www.leveretpublishing.com

Kyrgyzstan: Bishkek and Tien Shan
First published - July 2017
Published by
Leveret Publishing
56 Covent Garden, Cambridge, CB1 2HR, UK

ISBN 978-0-9957680-7-9

© Stephen Platt 2017

All rights reserved. No part of this publication may be reproduced, stored in a retrieval system or transmitted in any form by any means, electronic, mechanical, photocopying, recording or otherwise, except brief extracts for the purpose of review, without the written permission of the publisher.

Kyrgyzstan
Bishkek and Tien Shan

Kyrgyzstan 2013

Bishkek

Sunday 21 April

I meet Enrica in Stansted and we fly to Istanbul where we grab a sandwich and a beer and fly on to Bishkek. The plane is empty and I'm able to change seats and move next to Enrica. She has her earphones on and I get out my computer for the five-hour flight. At the airport there are lots of people in military uniform with big wide Russian hats but getting through customs and immigration is easy and our taxi driver is waiting for us. From the airport there is a wide boulevard lit by bright lights and lined with Willows with white painted trunks. Beyond the line of bright trees the night is black and the steppe rolls away into the distance with just the occasional light in a night sky full of stars. We have breakfast of soft cheese, olives and black tea and then to bed. It is 6am here and it is already light. I unpack and hang up my clothes, find my eyeshade and earplugs, and get into bed and go to sleep.

Manas airport, Bishkek, backdrop of Tien Shan mountains

Enrica and I arrive at Central-Asian Institute for Applied Geosciences (CAIAG)

Monday 22 April

I wake after four hours. John, Max and Mark are working over computers in the dining room. They want to see the cards I've made for the scenario planning game we are going to run later this week with emergency managers. So we pour over the game and I try to appear confident. We agree to go to institute and view the room this afternoon. I sleep again for an hour and am just awake when John calls to invite me to lunch. We walk to a shopping mall with Marc from GFZ Potsdam and Sergei, an engineer from Tajikistan working on another project. They order but I don't know what to have; I don't feel hungry. Sergei suggests rice, which is a good choice and I have green tea to

On the roof of the Institute looking towards the mountains

drink. We wander back to the hotel and take a taxi. The city sprawls out along wide potholed roads. The remnants of Soviet concrete panel apartment blocks stick up like sore thumbs amongst the lowrise timber steep roofed houses. It is springtime and the trees are bursting into fresh, green leaf.

We arrive at the Institute and climb stairs to the conference room and meet the Dinara and the people from the Institute. They seem shy and a little out of their depth. They look to me to direct operations so I suggest we arrange the tables for the three groups – events, decisions and information. I set up the camcorder and focus on the central decision table. We spread out the cards and take people through the start of the game. Everyone has questions and makes suggestions but the Institute people still look nervous until we get round the events table and I get them to sort the cards into the time periods and they begin to relax and get involved. I leave Dinara and Mark sorting. Dinara is a political scientist. She says she will just observe but I suggest she help me with the decision table and she agrees. There is some confusion about the interpreters. They are doing simultaneous translation on day one but during the game we want them to work with each group. Someone is

These apartments do not look as though they wiithstand an earthquake

on the phone complaining they can't do that, but it turns out they are only concerned about our not needing the equipment and assume we don't want to pay for it. I assure them that payment is not an issue. Everyone seems happy and confident about Thursday.

It is 5.30pm and Dinara has her coat on and wants to go but we ask to go up to the roof to get a view of the distant mountains covered in snow. The city is spread out around us – one million people on a flat plain stretching North towards Kazakhstan. We look over concrete apartment blocks. Roxanne comments that she doesn't think they would survive an earthquake because the panels would fall out. The concrete chimneys also look very rickety, being held on with metal straps. We talk about climbing; I want to go for a trek in the mountains. I say I plan to go to the Ala Archa National Park tomorrow and that I've arranged a car to pick me up at 8.30am tomorrow. John and Enrico say they'll come.

Max offers to take us to a restaurant down the road. He says, in his delightfully Italian way, it is, shall I say, a kind of crappy restaurant, although maybe that is not quite the right adjective, you can decide. He and Marc find

Hotel at the entrance to the Ala-Archa Park

it most amusing, so I assume this is something of a catchphrase. The restaurant is like a family house but the food is good and I have soup followed by kebab. We are chatting after the meal. It is nearly 10 o'clock and I notice all the other guests have left and the family are sprinkling the carpet with water and then sweeping it with a broom. So I suggest we go to bed.

Tuesday 23 April
The driver was prompt and we set off into the suburbs. There are quite a lot of half-finished houses. One side of the road seemed more established with cherry trees surrounding the houses but on the other side the plots are bare and surrounded by ugly block walls. The road climbs towards the snow-capped mountains. We come to a wide junction and the driver suddenly braked and we can see two cops in their wide brimmed hats pulling people over. We drive past slowly and the fat one signals with his pink button. Our driver is led off and climbs into the police car. He is away 10 minutes or so and comes back shaking his head and shrugging his shoulders. We didn't know if he'd had to pay a fine or a bribe or what had happened.

Walking into the Tien Shan

We paid the £2 park entrance fees and drove 12 km to a hotel where the paved road ended. The driver dropped us and we set off walking. It was chilly so I put on my pullover that I had remembered to bring at the last minute. I am rather ill-equipped, having forgot my trainers and only have my leather sandals for walking. Still I expect I'll manage. We consult the faded map near the hotel and decided to aim for a waterfall about 4 km away. Our path forked off to the left from the Jeep track that continued up the valley to a ski resort the guidebook said was out of action.

We walked in single file – Bjorn from Oslo, John and Enrica and me at the rear. We are at about 2,000m and I'm a bit out of breath with the altitude. We have to climb about 700m. I manage to keep up since we're going at a gentle pace. John spots an eagle soaring high above the valley. Winter is over and, although there is still plenty of snow, the trees – mainly spruce and beech – are green with new leaves and the wild flowers are out – pale iris, spiky ground orchid and delicate buttercups. Enrica says her family make liquor with them in Italy.

We arrive at some huge rocks and sit and share the oranges I brought and

Start of the Ala-Archa walk

Every couple of minutes a marmot pops up

admire the view. There is less water than one would expect given the size of the stream beds. Maybe the main melt has already happened.

The next stretch passes by an open pasture and Bjorn spots a marmot. The field is riddled with holes and now and again a marmot pops up and sits on a rock for a while to enjoy the warm sunshine. A large bird flies just over our heads. It's not an eagle, but it's big and fast. Later we see it again a realise it's a lammergeier vulture. We hear a rock fall and I spot one of the large horned Marco Polo sheep that are the emblem of the park pounding down a steep scree slope. It is not alone; there is a whole herd and they come gambling down knocking over stones and cross the glacier in the bottom of the valley and bound up the opposite side. Three eagles circling overhead are most interested. Perhaps they hope one of the sheep will miss its footing.

The path peters out and we scramble over boulders in the stream bed. Sandals are not ideal. Nor are they much good on hard packed snow in which I have to kick steps. But I manage with cold toes. We reach a point where there might be a waterfall under the snow. I figure it's further up the valley to the main waterfall but say nothing. We've had enough though. After a brief rest

Lammergeier vulture and Marco Polo sheep

Open toed sandals are not ideal footware for this terrain

and chocolate we set off back. We stop again at the marmot pasture and find a rock to shelter behind to have lunch. The sun has gone in, the wind has got up and it's chilly. I put on my anorak and its comfortable leaning against the rock and I nod off, half listening to a discussion about Bigfoot. It seems that the others have spotted a line of large footprints in the snow on the other side of the valley.

When we get back to the road a group of people are erecting a yurt and we stop and watch them for an hour or so. It's fascinating. An old woman directs operations. They have erected the wicker walls, a concertina of criss-crossed sticks, and are fitting the door. They want to get this right. If the door doesn't close well it is considered bad luck and they have to start again. They now have to raise the wagon-wheel centrepiece of the roof. After a false start they lashed two of the curve rafters together to make a fork and two men hold up the wheel, guiding it with embroidered tapes while the other men outside the ring of the wicker wall attempt to insert the curved slender rafters

Our high point – the frozen waterfall,

into sockets in its circumference. It is quite a business. The wheel twists, causing alarming cracking sounds and everyone exclaims and shouts advice to the two men holding up the wheel. Gradually the roof spars are fitted and then lashed to the wickerwork walls. Finally the old woman climbs the hillside to look down on the framework and must be satisfied because she starts unwrapping the brightly coloured reed mat that will cover the walls and uses the long tapes that where balancing the wheel to weave the roof spars together. It is cold and we don't have the patience to wait and see the hide covers stretched over the structure and our driver is waiting for us.

Back at the start of the walk they were erecting a yurt

We were too cold and our driver was waiting so we didn't see the final stage

We go out to eat together in the shopping mall. I choose an aubergine sauce and rice with a litre of Efes beer and am in bed by 9.30. Tomorrow we begin the real work. Max has designed in eight-page questionnaire to be applied at the end of the game. I think it's too long and some of the questions don't make sense. I'll try and tell him tomorrow

Wednesday 24th

A night of one terrible dream after another, filled with conflict and childish anger. My task today is to intrigue and captivate my audience, and to give them enough information about the structure and purpose of the game without frightening them off. The people at the Institute were very nervous and suspicious so it won't be easy. If it were me, I would want to know that I was in good hands and that the people running the game were properly prepared. Then I would need to be interested in the topic and open-minded about the idea of playing the game. Have people come willingly or have they been sent? Do they know each other already and have they worked together before? Or are they at loggerheads with each other – central and regional authorities; Tajik and Kyrgyz?

Part of the EU project SENSUM team

In the event it went quite well. The Kyrgyz and Tajik teams were waiting outside the hotel and we begin. To my surprise the simultaneous translation worked. One of the delegates in the Kyrgyz Ministry of Emergency, a man called Aibek seems to have elected himself spokesman and commented volubly on how they did things in Kyrgyzstan. It seems they still follow the protocols set in place by the Russian administration, but most of the systematic data collection and analysis seems to have gone by the board since independence and the current managers seem to have a fear of technology and science.

The batting order of speakers is Max talking about the EU SENSUM project, John talking about satellite imagery data and me talking about user information needs and how we devised the game. Then it is the turn of the Kyrgyz and Tajik disaster management people.

Almaz reads a solid presentation about the Kygyz system and then Shukrat explains the disaster management system in Tajikistan. It seems very bureaucratic. Aibek keeps interrupting, saying you said that before and let's get on with it. Shukrat is quiet and a little cowed by Aibek. The other Tajiks are calm and polite; perhaps they are used to it. Maybe it is a nationalistic thing or maybe hosts are always dominant. Or maybe it's just personality. I have been

Max introduces SENSUM

The team looks pensive, but we have done as much as we can to prepare

trying to find out about the 'Stans'. It seems relations with Tajikistan are okay but less good with Uzbekistan and Turkmenistan. This area was Turkish before it was Russian Soviet. Jamshed introduces himself as a Lieutenant colonel. He speaks about landslides and avalanches and again Aibek interrupts. He is quite rude. I ask for questions. Aibek says he has a lot, but it's all clear and they'll wait till tomorrow when they are playing the game. I say good idea and move on.

It's unfortunate that the head of the Institute isn't here or I might have asked him to chair the decision-making group, but now there is no alternative but to ask Aibek. Over lunch I grabbed an interpreter to help speak to Aibek. I draw a diagram showing the layout of the tables with decision-makers in the centre and information providers and events team either side. He objects and insist decision-makers should be at the beginning or the end of the line. He draws a pyramid with the decision-makers at the top and himself at the apex. I realise he sees my drawing of the tables as an organogram. It is going to be a laugh tomorrow. He enjoys making a joke and getting a rise out of people and his eyes screw up in his fat face as he shakes with laughter.

Dinner and vodka with Ulugbek, the jovial rector of the University

After lunch, while Max and Bjorn are speaking, I began to think about how to divide the groups. I knock up a slide assigning people to groups. Began the presentations and their wait until they're playing it tomorrow. I put the two people from the Red Crescent, who gave a presentation about work in the rural community schools, in the events group. Denis and the guy from UNDP, Marat, who was candid about their shortcomings, I put in the information team. But I realise that they may not come tomorrow because they slipped away early after lunch. So my careful planning is probably for nothing. We will have to sort it out in the first session. We finish early and I decide we will move the tables. We rearrange them so that the decision-makers are out of line with the other two tables, simulating Aibek's pyramid. The interpreters are interested. They have been very good at trying to understand the material and our needs and they offer to do simultaneous translation for each table, they say that they can use the various channels on their system to split the signals. We set up the microphones on the tables.

Everyone seems very pleased with the day and the participants are very jolly in the minibus going back to the hotel. I get a rest and we meet up to go out to dinner. Roxanne and James, her boyfriend, are here. They got in from China soon after nine and have been in the field all day surveying. The restaurant is a cut above the ones we have been going to. We sit at a long table. I'm in the middle of one side with Bjorn on one side and Roxane on the other. Ulugbek, the Rector of the University, at one end. He is a jolly man with a big smile. Sergei is nonplussed when Roxanne says she is a vegetarian. The meal is a cold meat platter followed by a plate of grilled meat.. All they seem to be able to provide Roxanne is extra salad. Max tucks in with gusto. We are on beers. The vodka arrives and Ulugbek makes a joke, telling Enrica that is the vodka is without gas since she announced earlier that she didn't drink and ostentatiously ordered water without gas. He obviously thinks it's uproarious. I knock one back and see the bottle go down. Ulugbek orders another and gets different people to give toasts. He encourages me to get up. Both Roxanne and Enrica are game to speak. I leave my glass full; it is the only way to avoid getting smashed. John and Max move places to be nearer the bottle and I regret not making more effort to be jolly but I need to pace myself for tomorrow.

I have a chat with Roxanne about whether I should stand as chairman again at CAR. She says I should and that she likes the way CAR operates and the direction it's moving in. I'm surprised and pleased. The toast continue. I have a chat with Bjorn about Norway and his work on landslides. Suddenly Roxanne jumps up and said she needs to get back. James says she wants to walk. I say I would go back with them if they were taking a taxi. So Ulugbek orders taxes for everyone. I jump in the first with Roxanne and James. We are in Central Asia. There is a full moon and the driver has a romantic Latin music playing in Spanish.

Thursday 25th of April
The day of the game; three months work on the line. We picked up the Ministry of Emergency people at their hotel. Outside, while we waited for them to appear, I spotted a timber two-storey house and went over to look at it carefully.

In the Institute we got out all the game materials, taped down the decision sheet and set up the camera. The participants filed in. I have decide to assign

Tradional timber house

the two most intelligent presenters from Kyrgyzstan and Tajikistan to the information table. But Aibek, the bossy one from yesterday, ordered two other people into the information group. I was slightly flummoxed. I realised it was likely that the people from Red Crescent were unlikely to turn up. So I grabbed one of the two guys Aibek has assigned to information. He was very reluctant to disobey, but I persisted. Max reminded me that we had planned to have a dry run. So I took them table by table beginning with the events. Aibek planted himself in the command chair at each table and grab the cards and shuffled them rather than try to understand them or arrange them into order as I had suggested. I wondered how it was all going to work with him taking such an obstructive role. I had tried flattering him by making him chairman, but this seemed to be backfiring. I showed them how the decision board logged all the information flows and decisions and how the time period changed and that they would get a break every 40 minutes and we kicked off.

The first session was very difficult. The man I put on the events table insisted on playing five cards at once, which might happen in reality, but completely overwhelmed the decision-makers. During the coffee break the

SENSUM team met to analyse what had gone wrong. The decision-makers had been frozen by the flood of events and had thrown the problem onto the information providers. But when I made the first set of cards I hadn't provided enough information about each event. I had expected the events team to provide this extra information about the location of the event, the source of the information and the likely consequences. But I had forgotten to explain this.

The second session went more smoothly and the information team wrote the extra information people needed on post-it notes attached to each card as it was played. But new problem emerged. The decision team needed information about the extent of the damage or the people affected, but failed to request this form the information team in a precise enough way. The information team gave an estimate of the time needed to produce information and the decision-makers just parked the decision rather than make a decision with inadequate information, as would happen in the real world. All this time Aibek either growled at the end of the table or went out for a smoke. An event card arrived saying there had been a major landslide

Aibek takes command, sorting the events cards into time sequence at the start of the game

and the main road from Bishkek into the interior was blocked. The decision team floundered. To prompt them I asked how they were getting search and rescue teams in to the region if the highway was blocked. Aibek said, in a cavalier way, by helicopter. What about the heavy machinery, I asked. We would build a new road was the answer.

One man seem to be taking charge of decision making and writing pink slips. I couldn't tell if they made sense because the translation was a little chaotic. The woman translating with the information team was good, but the man on our table had started behaving as if he was part of the team rather than just translating. Finally Max had a word with him and he was a little put out.

Two key events cards were played – the collapse of the hospital in an aftershock and a possible fracture in a dam. The decision makers failed to set up a temporary hospital and, when told by the information team that a thorough survey of the dam would take four weeks, they failed to order a quick survey or to establish if any population centres were vulnerable and, if so, to order an evacuation. The events team reported that the dam had burst with 8,000 casualties and a cholera epidemic had broken out with 500 cases on the first

The scenario planning game EVENTS team

day. The decision team had no temporary hospital or medical facilities in place, nor had they decided where to locate temporary camps, services or even ordered tents or shelters. Then the events group reported that severe cold weather had hit and winter had come early.

It was time for lunch and we were only halfway through month one. We decided not to hit them with any more events and cascading catastrophes, even though the events group had devised a scenario of winter rain and severe landslides. Instead we decided to provide an update about existing events and some good news about aid compensation, government support etc. We also decided to try and improve communication between the decision-makers and the information providers in the form of a Directive from the Prime Minister's office appointing an information minister to sit on the decision-makers board and act as a liaison. Aibek reacted amazingly. He point-blank refused to have this person appointed. He objected that this criticism of his team could not be tolerated. He point-blank refused to have this person appointed. He obviously saw the appointment as undermining his authority as chairman.

I try to get the quiet man Aibek had appointed to the information team

The INFORMATION team

to move across to the decision makers, but he looked terrified and locked rigid to his chair. It was a stand-off. Max explained that this was just a liaison role to improve communication but Aibek wasn't having it. During the play Aibek hadn't got involved in making decisions or directing discussion. He only seemed to pontificate, as if speaking to the media or sitting on a hostile committee and defending his territory. Maybe his role in real life is as attack dog and when anybody challenges his department's privileges or tries to interfere he goes into action. We let it go and got the game going again but from then for 20 minutes the decision makers seem to go on strike.

Then Almaz, the tubby one from Osh with gold teeth, who had given a solid presentation lumbered across and started taking the role, but in an informal way that worked, suggesting what information might be relevant and offering what he thought the information team could reasonably be expected to provide. He even suggested alternatives and asked which level of information decision makers wanted about camps – quick generalised information or detailed information that would take longer or somewhere between the two. The decision-makers looked lost. Aibek refuse to engage. Finally the man

The DECISION team

writing the decisions on the pink slips took the middle one like someone choosing a card at random from a spread deck.

We managed to play year one but when we got to year two and the offer of funding from the World Bank if they would write a development plan that prioritised projects they point-blank refused to discuss it saying it would be a commission's responsibility. I asked them to imagine that they were that commission. I even suggested the type of projects they might consider. But they insisted they were emergency management people and could think of no investment other than repair and rebuilding. So we decided to end the game there. I thanked them and said I wanted them to do one last piece of homework and fill in a questionnaire. Someone asked if they had to put their names on it. I said no, then wondered if that would mean Aibek and some of the others wouldn't complete it. I started taping down the post-it notes and cards on the decision-makers game board so they would stay in place when we folded the decision board.

Then we had a group photo. Everyone seemed pleased. There was an official thank you and the Ministry of Emergency personnel left to go to the hotel

Everyone seems very pleased with how it went

while we packed up and had a debriefing session. I was dog-tired and when they moved from discussing the game to whether or not we should try and locate events on a map I began to nod off.

We have been told by Dinara, who is organising everything, that we are going straight to dinner and that we will be dancing till 3am in the morning. We insist on going back to the hotel first and the driver offers to wait for us for half an hour. It is just time to shower and shave and change my clothes. The venue is a huge concrete pleasure dome on the edge of town. We pile through the front doors into what looks like a huge wedding with hundreds of guests at numbered tables and a man with a very loud PA system. It turns out that our dinner is in the basement round the side. The Xanadu with mountain views turns into a glitzy parking garage with live music.

We find our table and get stuck into salads as the vodka toasts begin. Then there is soup, which is extremely tasty, two kinds of bread, deep-fried profiteroles and round wheels with sesame seeds. The food is great. It is not clear if this is just the starter but I suspect there will be a main meaty course, so I go easy. Aibek is his usual bossy self, rearranging the tables. But the atmosphere is jolly and everyone relaxed and the vodka keeps coming of course. I'm asked to make a toast. I thank them for coming and wish them good fortune to be prosperous and the wisdom to cooperate with others. It's trite but it seems to go down all right. I slug back my vodka, forgetting to touch glasses with everyone. Nevermind. About 10 o'clock people start dancing Aibek drags Dinara's friend onto the floor. I'm feeling brave and since John, Erica, Bjorn and the others have gone dancing and I ask Dinara to dance. She says later maybe, but I insist. We all dance around in a group.

We are close to a party of eight girls and through the evening Aibek pushes us into dancing with them. There is a tall girl in a blue dress who takes a fancy to Max. We take a couple of short breaks and dance right through till 1 o'clock in the morning. Towards the end I get pushed into dancing with a brunette in a red dress who is a good dancer and I sense a circle has formed around us so I keep going. She dances close and bobs her head in the most provocative manner. I smile back, unsure if she's having me on. But despite my tired legs I'm on form and can match at twirls and twists and add steps of my own. A girl who Max says bit his ear runs her hand up my crotch as she dances past. The girl in the red dress simpers when I say goodbye. I dance with a blonde from the same group.

Jet setters clubbing Kygyz style

There is a move to leave so I go over to the party of girls and say goodbye and shake their hands and say how much I enjoyed meeting them. They asked my name but I can't hear there is so much noise. The two girls I danced with are both very friendly and attentive. It's nice. Dinara clears the table of uneaten food and fills four carrier bags, which I help her carry to a taxi. Then we are in the minibus heading back to the hotel and I'm quickly in bed.

Friday 26th of April
Despite everything I am awake early and first down to breakfast. Roxanne joins me after her run. She and James are taking the day off and going to Ala Archa. She shows me what they did yesterday in terms of the survey work. John is a little put out that she arrived on Wednesday morning and is taking the day off. But she has done the work and has checked the data, written up her report and made a PowerPoint already. She's a bit of a phenomenon. John says he's been speaking to his colleague in England and they have decided

alter the sample to try to capture unusual buildings. Roxanne is appalled and explains in no uncertain terms what she thinks this is a bad idea. One of the new areas they have chosen is miles away and the other doesn't guarantee finding any more unusual buildings than the original sample. I suggest to John that it is unwise generally to tinker with the sample and if you want to capture special buildings then you need local knowledge to identify them and then you can survey them separately and report separately. John seems unconvinced and uncomfortable with Roxanne's vehemence. Marc arrives so I give up my seat and sit at another table. Roxanne is right in my opinion. She says the purpose of the survey is to get a general overview of building stock in Bishkek and they have achieved this. But my god she is strident. Poor John. Somehow they reach an agreement. I go to my room. I work till 11 working out how to download the videos from yesterday. I am worried that the camcorder may only work with a PC. In fact it is quite easy when you attach the camera – Dropbox opens automatically and downloads all the files to a folder.

I set off the explore Bishkek

Soviet apartment block

I leave it running then go out walking east along Gorky Street to the commercial centre. But I have maps in both English and Russian I got from reception. I find a bench outside the commercial centre and sit and watch people. It is hot and sunny and a little humid because it rained yesterday. I turn

Bishkek town clock, A little like Harlow New Town

left on Sovietsky Street and cross the railway line in what looks like a massive central heating pipe underpass.

There are eight or nine story concrete apartment blocks. They must have been built in the Soviet era and some have interesting window detailing and

Children playing in the fountains

other design features. There are trams but most people seem travel in minibuses which arrive in a steady stream. Finally I get to at the centre. Across the road there is a square clock tower looks very Harlow New Town. I get out the map and work out where I am trying to get to before I dive down into

Man in traditional Kyrgyz hat

the underpass across the wide avenue.

The underpass is lined with stalls selling all manner of cheap goods. I'm aiming for the main department store called Zum just on the other side of the road. Two old men traditional white hats stand chatting and I surreptitiously

Zum department store

Opera house

Young couple taking their wedding photos in the park

snap them and then some children playing chicken running in and out of the fountains. It is very pleasant, friendly and human. It is lunchtime. The fountains are shaded by massive willow and there are benches with lots of people sitting enjoying the sunshine.

Zum is an old-fashioned emporium with dozens of glass-enclosed concessions on each of its six floors. The ground floor is dedicated to phones. On the fifth floor I spot a memory card for the camcorder and by dint of pointing managed to buy it. If it works it seems a bargain at about £8. I haven't got quite enough money but I make up the difference with a dollar and he accepts since there is a small profit in the exchange.

I walk round the Opera house again more faded glory. The parks that surround all the cultural buildings are treed and grassed and there are many sculptures of historical figures in the brutalist tradition. I stop often to rest on benches. I am tired from the late-night dancing. It is pleasant city in the sun watching the world go by. I spot a young couple in wedding outfits under the trees having their photograph taken by a friend. They look ridiculously young. She is in white with a veil and he is peering into a mirror from his iPhone and

Lenin points to a vanished past

trying to slick his fringe down. Finally they are ready and he puts on his jacket and they kiss for the camera.

The Museum of Modern Art is a rather imposing concrete building that might have graced Milton Keynes town centre seems permanently shut. Maybe there are no pictures left. There are paintings, however, in an open-air gallery running along the side of the park. But they're not really art. Mountain scenes seem most popular. There are striking portraits of Lenin and Marx that look as though they have been on sale a long time. There are mounted hunters with fur caps and eagles on their gloved fists and one of a semi-naked courtesan cuddling a lion.

   I finally find the rough-cast statue of Lenin I've heard about. It is huge and Lenin's outstretched arm is pointing to the golden future. It used to be outside the Museum of History pointing to the gilded domes of Ala-Too Square. But since independence Lenin has been moved here around the back and his place has been taken by a helmeted warrior mounted on a charger who must be some local hero like Genghis Khan. I climbed the steps of the Museum in two minds about whether I have the energy to walk round the exhibits but in the event I am turned away by a young lady cashier because I lack the entrance fee of about £2. Just as well. The outside tiling is falling off and I can see discarded piles of stuff through the dusty windows. History has clearly overtaken the Museum of History and the story the Soviet Union wanted to tell future generations. Two young soldiers in full dress uniform stand rigid in a glass box in the Square in front of the mounted warrior.

   I cross the wide avenue by a pedestrian crossing, timing my sally to coincide with traffic lights further down the road. I have noticed the traffic seems to respect pedestrian crossings if you are purposeful. I retrace my steps and take a pleasant park-like boulevard back south. It is slightly uphill and I rest a couple of times on convenient park benches. I watch young children on a school run doing a circuit of the park. They go fast. But on the second circuit after about half a mile most seem to break into a walk.

   My final rest is in front of the imposing railway station and its grand steps. There is a well-dressed drunk in a suit on my bench who gradually slumps forward and then sideways before slipping to the ground. It seems early for this level of stupor.

   The station has a big departure board. But only one train is displayed for later that afternoon. There is a long line of green carriages and beat-up blue diesel engine with curtains. A cross the railway by a footbridge and weave my way between the apartment blocks by way of parking areas and play squares. The apartments seem to be arranged into courtyards with trees, benches and play equipment for children. Again its rundown but very civilised. I tried

Only one train a day at this sleepy station

changing money in the station but the woman refuses to take my dollars. But the bank further down takes them so I have enough for a meal tonight.

I get to Gorky Street and am back in time to meet John. I take off my clothes and get into bed for a quick rest. I go down to the restaurant and work with him for a bit until its time to go out to a Turkish restaurant with Bjorn and Enrica. The restaurant is close but the catch is that everyone is smoking. The men are playing some kind of backgammon board game and passing a shisha pipe back and forth emitting clouds of aromatic smoke. We find a table at the back and order chicken and potato and cheese in a clay pot with rice on the side. I get back, pack my suitcase set the alarm for three.

Saturday 27 April
A rude awakening, followed by an alarming trip to the airport as the driver keeps nodding off and veering off the road. I am sitting next to him and move my hand towards the wheel which seems to jerk him awak l e. We go through three security checks and finally take off on our way to Istanbul and the next round in our scenario planning game with emergency managers in Turkey..

Milton Keynes UK
Ingram Content Group UK Ltd.
UKHW050610201223
434692UK00001B/7